BUG LIFE CYCLES

By Rod Barkman

DRAGONFLY

KidHaven PUBLISHING

Published in 2027 by
KidHaven Publishing, an Imprint of Greenhaven Publishing, LLC
2544 Clinton St., Buffalo, NY 14224

Written by: Rod Barkman
Edited by: Noah Leatherland
Designed by: Lucy Otter

All facts, statistics, web addresses, and URLs in this book were verified as valid and accurate at time of writing. No responsibility for any changes to external websites or references can be accepted by either the author or publisher.

Cataloging-in-Publication Data

Names: Barkman, Rod.
Title: Dragonfly / Rod Barkman.
Description: Buffalo, NY : KidHaven Publishing, 2027. | Series: Bug life cycles | Includes glossary and index.
Identifiers: ISBN 9781534571068 (pbk.) | ISBN 9781534571075 (library bound) | ISBN 9781534571082 (ebook)
Subjects: LCSH: Dragonflies--Juvenile literature. | Dragonflies--Life cycles--Juvenile literature.
Classification: LCC QL520.B37 2027 | DDC 595.733--dc23

Printed in China

CPSIA compliance information: Batch #QS27KH: For further information contact Greenhaven Publishing LLC at 1-844-317-7404.

Please visit our website, www.greenhavenpublishing.com. For a free color catalog of all our high-quality books, call toll free 1-844-317-7404 or fax 1-844-317-7405.

Find us on

PHOTO CREDITS
All images are courtesy of Shutterstock.com, unless otherwise stated.

Recurring – rachel epley design, Anastasiia Hevko. Cover – saeedahmad123. 4–5 – fizkes, Gelpi, pixelheadphoto digitalskillet, Prostock-studio, Studio 1One, wavebreakmedia. 6–7 – delayUH, Hatice Bakcepinar, Yevhenii Lukashuk. 8–9 – dreakrawi, Young Swee Ming. 10–11 – MR.AUKID PHUMSIRICHAT, Pierre Williot. 12–13 – Ernie Cooper, sucala. 14–15 –Matt Cole, Risto Puranen, TDROnline. 16–17 – Bob L Parker, Wirestock Creators. 18–19 – feathercollector, Tony Baggett, yoko_ken_chan, CC BY 4.0 < https://commons.wikimedia.org/wiki/File:Giant_Petaltail_f9_1169.jpg> via Wikimedia Commons. 20–21 – ART SUBLIMINA PHOTOGRAPHY, Filip Senigl. 22–23 – enginakyurt, Ernie Cooper, Figtography, song hakgo.

CONTENTS

Words that look like <u>this</u> can be found in the glossary on page 24.

A LOOK AT LIFE CYCLES

BABY TODDLER CHILD

All living things have a life cycle. A life cycle is all the stages of life a living thing goes through. This includes the beginning of life, growth, and, eventually, death.

The human life cycle begins with a baby, who grows into a toddler. Toddlers grow into children and then into teenagers. Teenagers grow into adults, who eventually become elderly people.

TEENAGER

Sometimes, adults choose to have children of their own.

ADULT

ELDERLY

MEET THE DRAGONFLY

Dragonflies are flying insects. Dragonflies have three main body parts. These are the head, thorax, and abdomen. Dragonflies also have six legs and five eyes. Their eyes allow them to see in almost every direction.

Dragonflies can be found all around the world, except for the continent of Antarctica. There are believed to be around 3,000 species of dragonflies worldwide.

Dragonflies are predators. They eat other insects to survive.

EGG

The life of a dragonfly begins when a female lays eggs in or near water. They may lay their eggs on the stems of plants or in large groups straight into still water.

an emperor dragonfly laying eggs in water

If it is warm enough, the eggs will hatch in one to five weeks. If eggs are laid in the fall, they may not hatch until the spring.

NYMPH

The baby dragonfly that breaks out of the egg is called a nymph. Nymphs shed their skin almost right away. Nymphs spend most of their time underwater as they grow.

Dragonfly nymphs have six legs, wing sheaths, and extendable jaws from the moment they hatch. They breathe underwater through a set of gills.

Dragonfly nymphs shed their skin up to 15 times before they reach their full size.

Dragonfly nymphs are predators. They hunt anything smaller than themselves, from other insects to small fish. Their extendable jaw shoots out at high speeds to catch prey.

Before becoming an adult, the nymph sits in shallow water and breathes air for the first time. When it is ready, the nymph leaves the water and climbs a nearby plant.

ADULT DRAGONFLY

When the dragonfly nymph sheds its skin for the final time, the adult dragonfly slowly emerges. The dragonfly straightens its abdomen and wings, then waits for them to harden before it flies for the first time.

Because its wings are still very weak, the new adult dragonfly isn't a very strong flier. It will not fly far. The stronger its wings become, the longer the dragonfly can fly.

New adult dragonflies are in danger of being caught by predators such as birds.

HOW DRAGONFLIES LIVE

Adult dragonflies usually live near fresh water, such as ponds, streams, and lakes. They have incredible eyesight and are one of the strongest flyers of all insects.

Dragonflies can reach speeds of 31 miles (50 km) per hour.

Dragonflies are some of the most successful predators on the planet. Thanks to their excellent eyesight and flying skills, they almost never miss their prey when they strike.

TYPES OF DRAGONFLIES

There are thousands of different types of dragonflies, and each one is unique. These are just a few of the amazing dragonflies that can be found around the world.

Dragonflies are some of the largest flying insects to have ever existed.

one of the world's largest dragonflies

mainly found in East Asia

END OF LIFE

As with all living things, a dragonfly's life will come to an end. They may become food for predators or simply die of old age. The dragonfly's short adult lifespan is spent finding a mate.

If the dragonfly has mated and the female dragonfly has laid eggs, then the nymphs that hatch from those eggs continue the life cycle.

LIFE CYCLE OF A DRAGONFLY

A dragonfly changes a lot during its life cycle. It starts its life in the water before zooming through the air as an adult.

The female dragonfly lays eggs in water. The nymph hatches. It grows, sheds its skin, and eventually climbs out of the water to shed one last time. Then it flies off to look for a mate.

GLOSSARY

emerges becomes visible by coming out or away from something

extendable can be made longer

gills organs that allow creatures to breathe underwater

hatch to break out of an egg

mate a partner (of the same species) that an animal chooses to produce young with

prey animals that are hunted by other animals for food

shed to remove and replace (the skin or shell) with another one that has grown underneath

species a group of very similar animals or plants that can make babies together

wing sheaths parts of the body of some animals that cover the wings

INDEX